Giraffes usually have only one baby at a time. They have to be protected from lions and leopards. So two or more adult females look after them in a kind of nursery, while their mothers are feeding. The giraffes live in groups, called herds.

Animals in the Wild

Giraffe

by Mary Hoffman

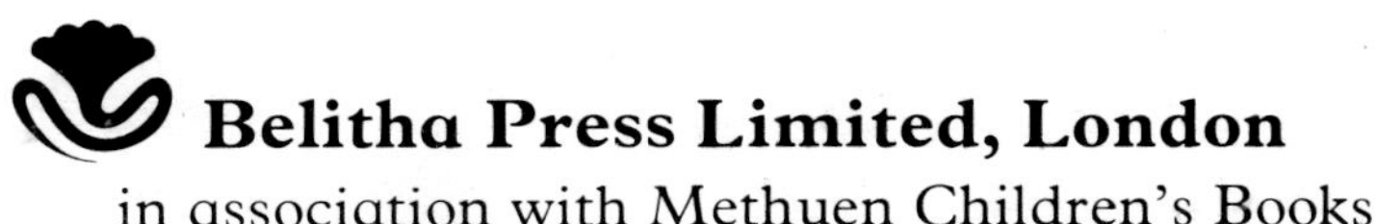

Belitha Press Limited, London
in association with Methuen Children's Books

The giraffe is the tallest animal in the world. A male can be six metres tall, including the neck. Even the babies are nearly two metres tall when they are born. They can stand after about twenty minutes. This one is probably a few days old.

There are twelve different patterns of giraffe. Animals of different patterns live in different parts of Africa.
This one is the common Masai giraffe, whose skin markings look like blotches.

This is a reticulated giraffe whose
dark patches are in the shape of a net.
It lives in Kenya.

Both male and female giraffes have short horns. The horns are covered with skin and hair. As well as the two you can see between the ears there is sometimes a second pair behind.

The giraffe has a very long tongue indeed.
It can stretch for nearly half a metre.
The tongue is very tough, which is important
when the giraffe feeds on thorny plants.

The favourite food of giraffes is the acacia tree. There are lots of thorns among its leaves and flowers. The giraffe wraps its tough tongue round the shoots, and softens them with its spit, so it can chew them.

You can see why the giraffe developed its enormous neck. It has the same number of bones in it as our necks – seven – but they are much bigger. Male giraffes feed at full-stretch and eat the leaves at the top. Female giraffes bend their heads and feed lower down.

Giraffes need to drink a lot, but it is
hard for them to reach the water.
While they are in their drinking position,
they could easily be attacked by lions,
so one of them keeps a lookout.

Giraffes do not get much rest. Sometimes they sleep standing up but usually they lie down and take five-minute naps. They have to stay alert in case of danger.

Herds all run at once when danger is spotted.
They can run quite fast – nearly 50km per hour.
Giraffes live in herds for safety, but the
herd does not always contain the same animals.

Giraffes are found in many parts of Africa.
There is no competition for their food,
because no other animal can reach the tree-tops.
These ones live near Mount Kilimanjaro in Kenya.

The giraffe has only one relation – the okapi.
This animal also lives in Africa, in the rain forests. It is very shy and it wasn't discovered by Europeans until 1900.
It lives by itself, not in herds.

Giraffes are quiet, peaceful animals. But young males sometimes practise fighting by necking . They wrap their necks round each other and push. It's a bit like wrestling.

Giraffes live easily with other animals. The largest number of giraffes live on the Masai Mara Reserve in Kenya. There are also large herds of gnu, who do not trouble the giraffe.

In zoos and wildlife parks you may see giraffe and zebra together. This is also common in the wild. Apart from lions and leopards, the giraffe's only enemies are people. But there is far less giraffe-hunting now than in the past.

Index

Useful words about giraffes

bull	a male giraffe
calf	a baby giraffe
cow	a female giraffe
herbivore	an animal that eats only plants
reticulated	having a skin pattern which looks like a net
ruminant	an animal that eats plants then regurgitates them and chews them again. Giraffes are ruminants.

Measurements

m = metre

km = kilometre

First published 1986 by Belitha Press Limited, 31 Newington Green, London N16 9PU in association with Methuen Children's Books Ltd, 11 New Fetter Lane, London EC4 4EE

Scientific Adviser: Dr Gwynne Vevers. Picture Researcher: Stella Martin. Design: Ken Hatherley
Acknowledgements are due to the following for the photographs used in this book:
Bruce Coleman Ltd pp. 2, 6, 9, 11, 12/13, 14, 15, 16/17, 18 and 21; Eric and David Hosking p. 8; Frank Lane Picture Agency Ltd 4/5 and 10; Natural Science Photos pp. 7 and 19; NHPA pp. 1 and 20; Oxford Scientific Films p. 3; Survival Anglia pp. 22/23.
Front and back covers: Bruce Coleman Ltd.
ISBN 0 416 96200 9 Printed in Singapore

Dedicated to Nicholas and Emily